SIX IMPOSSIBLE THINGS BEFORE BREAKFAST

Stories & Poems by
Norma Farber
Drawings by
Tomie De Paola
Charles Mikolaycak
Friso Henstra
Trina Schart Hyman
Lydia Dabcovich
Hilary Knight
▲▼Addison-Wesley

To Kathleen
who has made the
SIX IMPOSSIBLE THINGS
possible.

Text Copyright © 1977 by Norma Farber
Illustrations Copyright © 1977
by Addison-Wesley Publishing Co., Inc.
All Rights Reserved
Addison-Wesley Publishing Company, Inc.
Reading, Massachusetts 01867
Printed in the United States of America
ABCDEFGHIJK-WZ-7987

Library of Congress Cataloging in Publication Data

Farber, Norma.
  Six impossible things before breakfast.
  SUMMARY: four poems and two short stories about
unicorns, magic dough, and other fantastic things.
  [1. Fantasy. 2. Short stories. 3. American poetry]
I. De Paola, Thomas Anthony. II. Title.
PZ7.F2228Si   [Fic]   76-40264
ISBN 0-201-01969-8

Alice laughed. "There's no use trying," she said:
"one can't believe impossible things."
"I daresay you haven't had much practice," said the Queen.
"When I was your age I always did it for half-an-hour a day.
Why sometimes I've believed as many as
six impossible things before breakfast."

THROUGH THE LOOKING GLASS
Lewis Carroll

FLYAWAY DOUGH

drawing by
Tomie De Paola

1

One night a while ago, a baker mixed his usual batter of flour, milk, butter, sugar, salt and yeast, enough for twelve loaves of bread. He covered the bowl with a huge kitchen towel and set it in a draft-free corner of the kitchen. Then he sat down on the door stoop, as on many a mild night. He lighted his pipe and drew on it. The batter, snug in its enormous earthen bowl, filled gradually full of yeast bubbles.

In an hour or so the baker got up and stepped back into the kitchen. He stabbed the risen batter with his knife, *stab, stab, stab,* to release the bubbles. He added more flour, stirred the mix and turned out the shapeless dough onto a large breadboard, well powdered with flour. Then he buttered his hands and kneaded the mass with his strong baker's palms and fingers.

When the dough felt just right, silken smooth, he put it back into the freshly buttered bowl. In an hour or two, after this second rising, he would turn out the dough again and beat it hard with the flat of his hand. Then he would cut the wide thin mass into twelve slices, roll the slices into loaves, and let them rise again, each in its own buttered baking pan. That would be the third and last rising.

But during the second rising, that night a while ago, the baker once again sauntered out of his kitchen to get another breath of fresh moonlit air. He thought he'd even take a little stroll, a *very* little stroll.

The night was so lovely, so shining, so bewitching, he kept on strolling, strolling, strolling, with the fresh spring wind blowing against him. With each easy step he strayed farther and farther away from his bakery, his bowl, his pans, his oven. With each breath of fresh balmy air his thoughts strayed farther from the clock on the kitchen wall and the half-finished bread it was watching.

The moon beamed round and gold as a nearly-baked bun.

"What a pleasure it would be," the baker thought, "to scatter stars like sesame seeds all over the top of that great bun!" The baker almost imagined he could smell a heavenly, fresh-baked fragrance. He knew such a fragrance couldn't be, but he wandered on, more and more moonstruck, you might say, by the glow of that moon-bread. He liked to think of it as having been lifted, in the pan, from some giant oven in the sky.

"How proud I'd be to bake such a bread, big and beautiful as the moon!" he said out loud.

He sauntered along, taking an occasional dance step. And he played in his head with notions of bread and magic and moons and mighty baker-men — as a juggler might play with Indian clubs. He smiled as he sauntered.

Meanwhile, the dough in its own earthen bowl back at the bakery was rising up and up and up and out of its container, quite as easily as the moon had risen over the rim of the horizon. Up and out of the bowl the swollen dough kept growing, spreading a strong yeasty smell the length and breadth of the baker's kitchen, and even

beyond, through windows and doors and chimney, and down the cellar stairs. The fragrance spiraled into the night like an invisible vine.

The dough itself became airier, airier, as the yeast continued its warm bubbly work. Presently the whole doughy mass rose clear of the bowl and floated like a cloudy-white balloon out the door and into the moonlit dark. It had to *squeeeeeeeeze* through the doorway — it was already so large. It hovered a while over the WELCOME mat, then rose to the height of the low roof. And all the while it swelled, little by little by little, bubble by bubble by bubble. It floated up beside a tall poplar tree, missing the pointed leaves by inches. Riding on the breeze, the dough sailed off farther and farther from where the baker was wandering. Which was why he didn't see it. Or even smell it.

The dough drifted higher as the yeast fermented and new air-pockets formed. It rose high enough to startle the Wise Old Man in the Moon — and he is not easily startled.

"It can't be another moon," he assured himself. "Couldn't be. No such forecast. I'll just have a look through my glass."

He picked up his telescope, which had a very powerful moon-shaped lens. He peered. What he saw was a great object of dough, moon-shaped, or beachball-shaped, puffy with bubbles all the way through and growing and growing, second by second by second.

"Ho! It won't do!" harrumphed The Man in the

Moon. "People won't be able to see me from certain directions with this pasty pretender in the way!"

It was true. At that very moment the natives of a certain desert kingdom back on the earth thought they were watching a total eclipse of the moon!

The Man in the Moon lost no time. He summoned his neighbors, the stars.

"This unbaked upstart has no business taking up a bigger and bigger and higher and higher place in the universe." He reasoned calmly, "Why it's casting a shadow on those of us who belong here and have jobs to do. It's just not natural. Let's tickle the wind out of the ambitious, overleavened loaf."

With that, the stars, always ready for a good joke, pointed hundreds of needly star-fine fingers at the pasty mock moon. They pricked and poked and tickled. In no time at all, bubbles began to escape from the dough in a hundred hissing places. And then in another hundred. And another. The starry fingers kept pricking until they'd quite taken the wind out — all of it.

The dough was deflated. It plummeted from the heavens in a kind of crooked whirling dance, looking very much like a mammoth flying pizza.

The baker, still strolling into the wind, heard a low whistling in the quiet night air. He turned to look and gasped, "A Flying Saucer!" What a night of strangenesses. It was getting late. He hurried back to finish his baking — a longer distance than he remembered having come.

He went directly to the great earthen bowl where he had left the dough, rising for the second time. "What's this?" he gasped in astonishment. The empty container stared back at him, and of course no one answered. The clock on the wall kept ticking as usual. "After midnight!" the baker groaned. "I'd better make a fresh batch!"

Without further ado he mixed a new batter and set it in a draft-free corner to rise. This time he stayed right in the middle of his kitchen the whole rising-time — all three rising-times. Nothing could have budged him from that kitchen. And he stayed right through the baking time of the dozen loaves. He never once took his eyes off the oven.

And when the first customer came to buy bread in the morning, the first golden loaf was just ready to be lifted out of the oven and shaken very gently from its pan. The baker warned, "Take care. This bread is hotter than usual."

Perhaps you're wondering about that first batch, that flyaway dough?

It whirled and whirled, crookedly, falling and falling, till it plunged into a warm duck pond not a mile from the baker's door. The flat round mass simmered like a dumpling, and all the pond creatures, the waterworms and spiders and striders and boatmen, the winkles and snails and limpets and crayfish, the sponges and mites and scuds and mayflies — everyone had a flyaway fall-down feast.

I SADDLED MY UNICORN

drawing by
Charles Mikolaycak

2

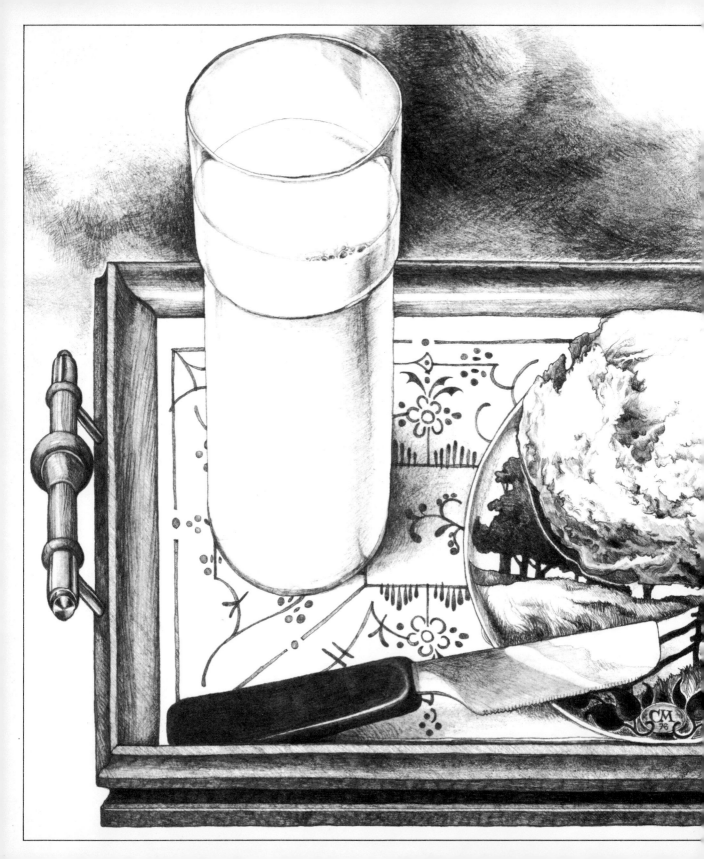

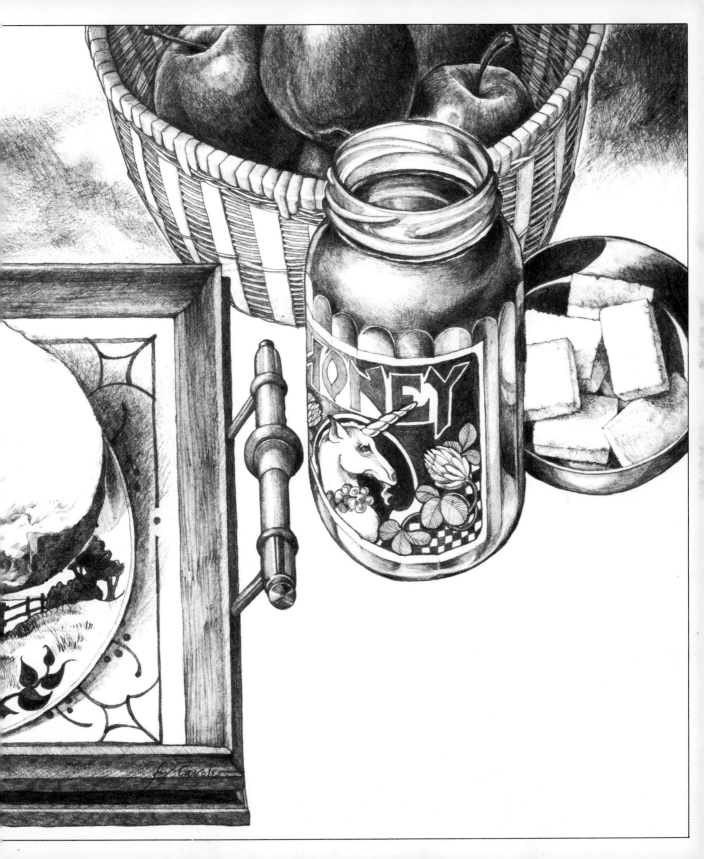

I saddled my unicorn early one day.
I thought I would mount him and gallop away.

I thought I would ride him an hour or two,
through meadows a-plenty and villages few.

I thought I would ride him two hours or three
by brooklets and rivers that flow to the sea.

I thought I would ride him three hours or four
through dust of the roadside and dunes of the shore.
And if he was willing I'd ride him still more.

I saddled my unicorn — hoping to ride.
My unicorn looked at me sideways, and shied.

One foot in the stirrup, I sprang in the air.
But when I got seated — my steed wasn't there.

My steed wasn't there, and myself in the dirt
lay tumbled and wondering where I most hurt.

My steed wasn't there. He was inches away,
pretending to sniff at a bundle of hay.
I called him to come and he came with a neigh.

I gave him some sugar. He licked at my palm.
He looked most affectionate, fearless, and calm.

I polished his horn with the tail of my shirt.
I flicked from his flank a few smidgeons of dirt.

I brushed out his tail to make sure it would fly
as wild as the windiest cloud in the sky.

And up then I mounted. His horn in my hand,
I sprang from the ground, in the saddle to land.
To land in the saddle was what I had planned.

But where I arrived, with a thump and a thud,
was *smack*! in the midst of a puddle of mud.

I opened my hand; it was holding no horn.
My hair was in tangles. My kerchief was gone.

I took a deep breath. Then I counted to ten.
I swallowed hard, once. Then I stood up again.

I opened the buckle and loosened the cinch —
that fastened his saddle — an inch or half-inch
in case the belt happened to press him, or pinch.

Then I mounted. Hurrah! Oh I really hung on!
There I was in the saddle! My steed, though, was gone.

There I sat in the saddle. I rode on the floor.
My unicorn cropped a white flower by the door.

Getting up, pretty angry from fall after fall,
I guided my unicorn back to his stall.

I started to lock up the stable. But no!
A wind swept the hay-loft. It spun to and fro.
It whistled like sirens, and called us to go.

He folded his foreleg. He knelt by my side,
as if he would say, "Here's my back, won't you ride?"

And suddenly, clearly, I now understood
what I hadn't known sooner — though everyone should.

A unicorn's different. A burro or horse
considers his saddle a matter of course.

A unicorn's made for the lightness of air.
A saddle is more than his freedom can wear.
But straddle him *bareback* — he'll go anywhere!

I gave him an apple to tell him I knew.
I straddled him lightly, and oh how we flew.

We galloped and galloped, two hours or three,
by brooklets and rivers that flow to the sea.

We galloped and galloped, three hours or four,
through dust of the roadside and dunes of the shore.

We galloped and galloped and galloped away
by hill and by hollow, by forest and bay.
We never came back till the finish of day.

"I WISH" SAID MRS. GILLIGAN

drawing by
Friso Henstra

3

"I wish," said Mrs. Gilligan, sitting huddled in her rocking chair on that dismal, dark, bitter-cold winter's day, "bubbles wouldn't burst."

Someone Up There must have heard her. For the very next bubble she blew off the bubble wand — aaah! — stayed plump and perfect, not ever breaking, as it rose slowly, slowly, slowly, to the kitchen ceiling — there to rest like a lighter-than-air balloon.

"I wish," said Mrs. Gilligan, "I could do that again." She blew another bubble, perfect and whole as the first. It too rose and rested at the ceiling. She rocked with delight.

She kept wishing and blowing. She blew a third bubble, firm and unbreaking, and called her dog to come see it. He rose on his hind legs and nuzzled it in mid-air. Even so, it didn't burst. So the third bubble joined the first and second way up against the ceiling.

Mrs. Gilligan hugged her dog. "I wish," said Mrs. Gilligan, "I could fill this moldy old kitchen with bubbles." So she blew on her bubble-wand, a long steady breath, making seven at a blow. They rose as if on wings and found places against the ceiling. When she clapped her hands with pleasure, several more bubbles bounced off the wand and spiraled their way upward.

In no time at all — which is to say, in the time it takes to sing *I'm Forever Blowing Bubbles* — the ceiling was layered with a row of many-colored spheres, shining like the finest crystal. The firelight flickered rainbows on each globe. "It's like a palace," said Mrs. Gilligan. And she dipped her wand in soapsuds and blew a second layer of bubbles close up against the first. The cat stretched, yawned and shook herself, and sprang down from the mantel. Her fur got a little wet where a bubble grazed her. A damp diamond glistened at the end of one whisker.

And still Mrs. Gilligan blew.

The parrot in his cage squawked. He stuck his bill between the bars and tried to puncture the bubbles as they passed. But they simply squirmed a little and continued floating upward.

One bubble settled against a spider web, finely spun into lace in a high corner. The spider crawled all over the bubble, up and down and around. Another bubble floated up behind her and squeezed her. She scuttled down the wall into a hole in the floor.

"I'm glad," said Mrs. Gilligan, "to change this dull kitchen into dazzling bubbles." So she blew and blew and blew till the room was half filled — the upper half — with the shining spheres. The parrot squawked and lifted his feet — left, right, left, right, madly — while several small bubbles drifted between the bars onto his perch and into his dish.

"Out you go," said Mrs. Gilligan, as she unhooked his cage and placed it on the front stoop. She never for a moment stopped blowing. The cat slunk out after her onto the stoop. The dog followed the cat. The three pets huddled together in the cold. Mrs. Gilligan turned her back, went into the kitchen and banged the door shut.

Minute after minute after minute, Mrs. Gilligan blew her kitchen full of bubbles. They settled on her head and shoulders, and squished up against her comfortable body. A mouse took one look, backed into a hole and barricaded it with splinters.

Mrs. Gilligan rocked and blew, and blew and rocked, till the whole room was tight as a drum with bubbles. The fire on the hearth hissed and died under bubbles. Mrs. Gilligan's chair was wedged motionless with bubbles.

Out on the stoop under the blackening sky, the cat and the dog and the parrot shivered against one another in the cold and called out crossly to their mistress. The wind was blowing up a storm. The sky turned pitch black. But Mrs. Gilligan was too busy to notice, blowing just one more bubble, and just one more bubble, filling the closets, the cupboards, the drawers cram full!

Crash! went a windowpane as the fury of the wind blew it in. And *bang*! went the door as the angry gusts swept thousands of bubbles against it and blew it out.

Whoosh! went Mrs. Gilligan, as masses of bubbles pushed against her, and she too was blown out, light as a bubble herself, and bubble-wand in hand. She landed with a *cloomp*! in a pile of compost in the corner of the yard.

Climp! *climp*! *climp*! landed her pets beside her. They dug themselves in as deep as they could. She wrapped her arms around them. She patted them snug into their holes. "I wish," said Mrs. Gilligan, "I'd never wished."

There was a hissing like rockets. Bubbles spun out of the kitchen and whirred all around the yard, dancing like dervishes, then shooting up into the air like kites. Bubble after bubble after bubble, they kept blowing out of the house, while Mrs. Gilligan and her pets huddled for dear life in the compost heap. In her hand she clutched a broken bubble wand.

When the last glossy bubble twirled dizzily once and veered away, the mouse tiptoed out onto the stoop and looked around.

Mrs. Gilligan dug herself out of the compost and brushed herself off. Dog, cat and parrot dug themselves out and followed her back into the house.

The kitchen was a shambles. But at least there wasn't a single bubble — not one — left hovering on the ceiling. The spider was up in her corner, as usual. She was quite busy mending her web.

"I wish," said Mrs. Gilligan, as she set out seed for the parrot, milk for the cat and a meaty bone for the dog, "I wish you'd forgive my silly wishing."

Through the broken windowpane a full moon shone down into the kitchen.

"Now," said Mrs. Gilligan, "*there's* a silver-bright, everlasting bubble for you!"

HERMAN A. SIMONDS AND THE SEVEN-MILE ROAD

drawing by
Trina Schart Hyman

4

Talk about blizzards,
talk about snow,
talk about temperatures
forty-odd below.

Talk about heroes,
say Casey Jones,
sing Paul Bunyan
and other well-knowns.

But save ammunition,
let it explode
for Herman A. Simonds
and his Seven-Mile Road.

Season was December,
bitter to behold:
winters up in Michigan
get mighty cold.

Snow began at daybreak,
fell through the gloom;
I'd better, said Herman,
be getting on home.

Started up his truck,
and the snow it snowed.
Turned on his lights,
couldn't see the road.

Old Noah had an Ark,
when *his* trouble struck.
Herman had a shelter
tacked on his truck.

He fried him some eggs,
ate them on bread,
fueled up his stove,
went right to bed.

Woke up fresh,
perky as a toad,
lifted out his shovel,
to clear him a road.

Heaped that shovel
full as a hod,
inched up his truck
a quarter of a rod.

Rested a while,
ate sardines,
slept a few hours,
had sweet dreams.

Didn't once figure
a chance of being towed:
not Herman A. Simonds
of the Seven-Mile Road.

Shoveled through evening,
shoveled all night,
didn't stop shoveling
till morning light.

Shoveled and thawed,
settled down to doze;
woke up fast
when he almost froze.

Day after day,
load after load,
had to keep clearing
that Seven-Mile Road.

Never saw a soul,
never heard a sound.
Shoveled and sweated off
twenty-five pound.

Shoveled to get warm,
and to keep him alive.
Felt like a million,
was sixty-five.

Worked like a woodsman
cutting up a load;
cleared not a path
but a Seven-Mile Road.

Talk about blizzards,
talk about snow,
talk about men
with git-up-and-go.

You can have your heroes,
keep your tales
of swingers of sledges,
riders of rails.

But give me the man
with the genuine goods:
shoveled half a month
out of Michigan woods.

Didn't need to holler,
didn't have to cry,
didn't want to lay
right down and die.

Took up his shovel
in hand and showed
how a guy goes to town
without being towed . . .

if he's Herman A. Simonds
on the Seven-Mile Road.

ON A CERTAIN RAINY FRIDAY

drawing by
Lydia Dabcovich

5

On a certain rainy Friday
afternoon in wet November,
several hours still to sundown,
there goes Mrs. Molly Manning
in the Number 6 bus.
There she goes with green umbrella,
totes a purple shopping basket,
rides a certain rainy distance
down to where she likes to market
in a certain corner store.

On that certain rainy Friday
afternoon in wet Manhattan,
there goes Mrs. Molly Manning
to the fruit and salad counter.
O the apples look so luscious,
she must buy at least a dozen.
So she starts to put some apples
in her purple shopping basket —
when she finds it isn't *there*! —
on her arm where she had placed it
when she started out to market
in that Number 6 bus.

Out she dashes on that Friday
into fairly wet Manhattan
where the bus has gone a distance,
every moment getting smaller,
every moment driving farther
with that purple shopping basket
which a certain Mrs. Manning
left behind her when she left.

On a certain rainy Friday
afternoon in wet Manhattan
when it won't be long to sundown,
you can seldom find a taxi
though you need it very badly
if you plan to catch the bus
where you left a purple basket.
So you stand with your umbrella
like a parachute above you
as does Mrs. Molly Manning
till a kindly, bearded fellow
stops his racing car beside her.
"May I help you?" then he says.

So she tells him all her trouble,
and he cries, "Let's find the basket!"
Well, she takes his invitation
and together in the rain
off they go down rainy Broadway
in a hot but wet pursuit
of that bus (that has the basket)
disappearing, disappeared.

Well, this kindly, bearded fellow
has a way of stopping buses:
simply pulling right in front!
See how fast he cuts them off,
and persuades them to the curb!
At which point our Mrs. Manning
leaves the car and climbs the bus.

Is it *this* one she was riding?
Can she find her purple basket?
Sorry, no. Let's try another.
And another. Then another.

Here are *three* the bearded fellow
pulls in front of, *three together*!
Quick, get out, get on! They're stopping!
One. Two. Three. And still no basket.

Well, the day is growing dimmer
on that certain rainy Friday,
getting closer now to sundown.
And the kindly, bearded fellow
who is Jewish and a rabbi
says they'll find her purple basket,
yes, they'll find it very shortly
for he has to be in Brooklyn
by the very stroke of sundown.
"Out you go! I've stopped another!"

But no basket. Not much longer
and the day will sink to sundown.
What to do? It's getting darker.
Where to go? To 54th,
where the buses are garaged?
It's a long chance, and our last.

Here we are, and Mrs. Manning
in less time than takes to tell it
finds the busy bus-dispatcher
in his office. "Have you found it?
Have you found my purple basket?"

"Here it is!" Hooray, hooray!
Filled to brimming with red apples,
just the kind she would have bought
if she'd had her purple basket
when she saw them in the market,
such amazing Mackintoshes,
why, a dozen, no, eighteen!

Hurry, Mrs. Molly Manning!
For it's darker and still darker
on this certain rainy Friday,
only minutes now to sundown
when the sundown comes to Brooklyn.

Well, they munch on rosy apples
while that kindly, bearded fellow
drives her home and waves goodbye —
just in time to drive to Brooklyn,
only seconds now to sundown,
on that certain rainy Friday
afternoon in wet Manhattan
when a purple shopping basket
first is lost and then is found,
and the rain — just look! — has stopped,
and the sun's a rosy apple
eaten up by hungry dark.

TO CHEER AN UNHAPPY PRINCESS

drawing by
Hilary Knight

6

Tomorrow you shall drive to town.
Your carriage shall be beetle-brown
with seats of velvet coxcomb-red.
You'll wear a wreath upon your head.
Your belt shall be a chain of gold,
with buckle a sunburst to behold,
your cloak the whitest in the land,
with six-inch hem of ermine band.
Four Spanish ponies, unsurpassed
for splendid plumes, shall pull you fast.
You shall have flute, guitar, and song
as lively as the day is long.

> *Thank you, father, for telling me.*
> *But I'm unhappy as I can be.*

You shall have cider freshly pressed
from apples famous for their zest.
You shall have crisp potato chips,
salty on tongue and teeth and lips,
and feasts of peas and plums and steak,
followed by sherbert, nuts and cake,
and lollypops and jelly-beans
and honey-nougats fit for queens.

> *Thank you, father, for telling me.*
> *I'm still unhappy as I can be.*

Three hounds shall follow where you ride,
and deer and doe run close beside,
and bugles blow their sweetest art
to drive the sadness from your heart.
Your servants, numbering twenty-four,
shall pitch a tent upon the shore,
and raise a banner sewn with fire
and set with emerald and sapphire.
You'll sit upon your throne of light,
with parrots perched to left and right.
The far-come nightingale will stay
to serenade you night and day.

> *Thank you, father, but you'll agree*
> *I'm quite as sad as I can be.*

For you the sunset shall be dawn.
For you the drawbridge shall be drawn,
for you a barge quite gently splash
with four and twenty oars of ash.
Your crew shall cook and sing and row:
"O hey, and how, and rumblylowe!"
while forty torches burning high
ignite the starry lamps of sky.

> *Thank you, father. But can't you see*
> *I'm still unhappy as I can be?*

Upon a certain splendid day
you'll reach your palace, there to stay.
Into your chamber you'll be led,
to see your lovely bridal bed,
with hangings made of white and blue,
bedecked with lilies fresh as dew,
silk curtains pleated fold on fold,
and bedposts fourteen-carat gold,
With canopy to cap your head,
curtains with parrots white and red,
and quilts of ermine, hard to find,
inlaid with jewels, the costliest kind.
Your room shall rise three stories high,
a roof of crystal frame the sky.

> *Thank you, father. But can't you see*
> *I'm sadder than I can bear to be?*

When the first rooster wakes the land,
a prince shall take your sleeping hand
and tell you sweetly that and this,
and ask you only for a kiss.
And all his time shall then be spent
cheering you from your discontent.

> *O thank you, father! Say no more!*
> *I've never been quite so glad before!*

WHAT I DO BEFORE BREAKFAST

Norma Farber
I walk to an eastern window and watch the cardinal-red sun inch up between skyscrapers — quite like one of Mrs. Gilligan's bubbles.

"Impossible!" I tell myself. And yet there it is. Even changing magically while I watch. To so brilliant a great gold coin I can't stare at it any longer. "Well," I conclude. "If sunrise is possible — anything's possible. Even the *im*possible!" And with that, I turn and fix breakfast: orange juice the color of an oriole's breast, egg, yellow-hearted as a daisy with surrounding white of petals, coffee, the rich dark loam of this impossibly good earth we live on.

Tomie De Paola
I make it a solemn rule never to do *anything* before breakfast.

Charles Mikolaycak
For me, breakfast is the best meal of the day, so I try to save it for lunch. Therefore, I do many things before having it. Like feeding the cats theirs, reading papers, taking bus rides, sharpening pencils and maybe even having a pre-breakfast breakfast. Sometimes I even have breakfast at dinner.

Friso Henstra
I scratch my back some, then take a cautious look at the picture I drew the night before. After that, I usually stare off into the sky for a long time.

Trina Schart Hyman
9:30 A.M. Brush teeth. Sit on toilet and read ads from *The New Yorker*. Shower. Put on (in this order) deodorant, Yardley's Lavender Cologne, purple eye shadow, black eye liner, clean shirt, underpants, blue jeans, sneakers, eyeglasses. Exchange pleasantries with my friend Dilys. Go downstairs. Feed cats Tender Vittles. Look at last night's drawing effort. Let the dogs in. Fill the tea kettle with water and light the gas stove. Answer the telephone. 10:30 A.M.

Lydia Dabcovich
I have to do two impossible things before breakfast. The first is to wake up. The second is to get up.

Hilary Knight
I open my eyes. There's something fluffy stirring at my feet. It's Fatima, my personal alarm clock and cat model. I give her a mutually satisfying toe massage, think about yesterday's events and non-events, last night's dreams and today's breakfast. Fatima and I settle on and finish off a dish of mutually satisfying kippers and plunge into work.

"Fatima! Whiskers a little to the right."